ONE LAST LITTLE PEEK, 1980-1995

Books by Berkeley Breathed

ONE LAST LITTLE PEEK, 1980-1995

The Final Strips, the Special Hits, the Inside Tips

BERKELEY BREATHED

L|B
1837

Little, Brown and Company
Boston New York Toronto London

FIRST EDITION

Library of Congress Cataloging-in-Publication Data

Breathed, Berke.
   [*Outland*. Selections]
   One last little peek. 1980–1995 : the final strips, the special
hits, the inside tips / Berkeley Breathed. — 1st ed.
     p. cm.
   Selections chiefly from the author's *Outland* comic strip, with some
selections from his *Bloom County* strip.
   ISBN 0-316-10690-9
   I. Breathed, Berke. Bloom County. Selections. II. Title.
PN6728.092B75 1995
741.5'973 — dc20   95-17453

10 9 8 7 6 5 4 3 2 1

KP

Published simultaneously in Canada by Little, Brown & Company (Canada) Limited
Printed in the United States of America

INTRODUCTION

two surprises for me upon the completion of the Opus and Bill story: first, the drawing of the last *Outland* strip proved more depressing than I had expected. Second, while reviewing the cartoons from the entire fifteen years of *Bloom County* and *Outland* for this book, I was taken aback by how reasonably good the first few years of *Bloom County* actually were.

I have always been my most damning critic. I usually avoided reading my older cartoons simply because to me they were too often disappointments. Many had been drawn in the throes of a sleepless, manic, forty-hour 'tooning binge — typical of my work habits before a vague sense of professionalism and encroaching middle age stopped such things. And what seems funny to a sleep-deprived brain at 4:00 A.M. often reads as merely hallucinogenic when laid down on the sober newsprint of a newspaper comic page. This may explain my initial popularity on college campuses around the country.

But after recent review, the work from the early days seems to have weathered the years pretty well, actually. Yes, overwritten, over-wordy, underfocused, and occasionally *Doonesbury*esque . . . but still fresh and inventive. Maybe it's brashness that I'm seeing. Or brash-ness before *everyone* was brash. Anyway, I recently found myself smiling, even chuckling, at a few of these early, amateur efforts, which surprised me. Maybe it was the cleansing distance fifteen years provides. Or maybe in those old strips I recognize the hungry stripper of the early nineteen-eighties working against deadline at four in the morning, sleepy eyelids held open with masking tape (true) and hoping like mad that the *Chicago Sun-Times* wouldn't cancel that week. (They finally did, twelve years later. The louts *always* were touchy.) Maybe I laughed recently in the bittersweet knowledge that the ambitious little smart aleck was gone forever, permanently replaced by what we all become in the Funny Papers: a lifer. Complacent, lazy, coddled, sexually harassed by groupies, impossible to fire, and sometimes wealthy . . . but not hungry.

Eventually the work suffers, of course. The *really* scary dinosaurs aren't in *Calvin and Hobbes*; they're scattered around the rest of the page, ancient, unmovable, and dodging extinction. Some of the better TV series have left the party while they were still having fun. It seems reasonable that cartoonists show the same good sense. Which leaves nothing left to say but goodbye. It has been my privilege.

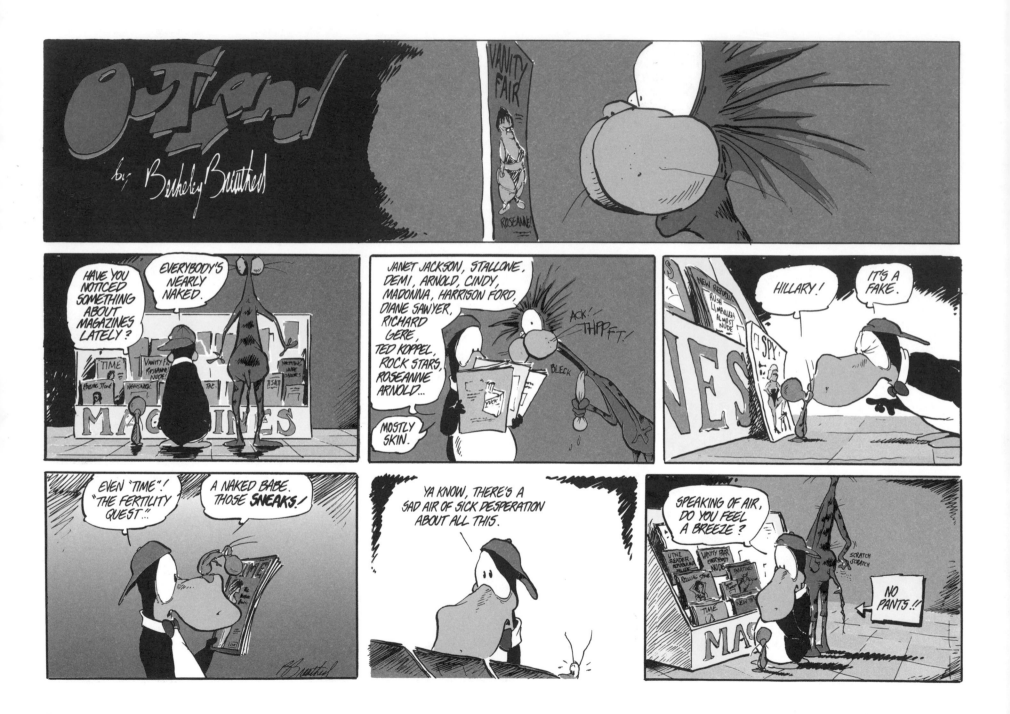

Outland
by Berkeley Breathed
THAT'S IT!!...
SORRY, SHINY COLD WORLD. BUT I'M A-PULLIN' OFF THAT STUPID SUPER INFO-FREEWAY DATA HIGHWAY THINGAMAJIG...
...AND RETIRING TO RELISH THE GLORIOUS NATURAL ORDER OF THINGS...
...THINGS UNFLETTERED WITH ARTIFICIAL COMBOBULATION!
POING
POING
POING
LO, I AM REBORN: "DANDO, THE DANDELION BOY"!
FWOOMP!!
GOT A PHONE JACK NEARBY?
OO...BABY, YEAH...THIS IS GOOD! I'M GOOD!...
WELCOME TO DANDELION INTERNET
VIRTUAL DANDELION
MIAMI
BOSTON
MOSCOW
"DANDO" DOES ELECTRONS.
B Breathed

Outland
by Berkeley Breathed
ZIP!
MILQUETOAST HAS ANOTHER EPIPHANY!
BROTHERS! FOR 20 MILLION YEARS, MALES HAVE BEEN DOIN' THE ASKING, AND BABES HAVE BEEN DOIN' THE DECIDING!!
MEN'S CLUB
WELL, WE'RE FED UP!! FOR NOW ON, THEY'LL DO THE ASKING... WE'LL DO THE DECIDING!!
YEAH!
THPPT!
HEE.. HEE.. HEE HEE
HEE HEE ACK
COME, BROTHERS... THE REVOLUTION STARTS TODAY!
B Breathed
ASK AWAY, LADIES... AND MAYBE WE'LL DECIDE!
ANYTHING DECIDED, BOYS?
YES. IT'S NOT TOO LATE TO CALL "1-900-HOT LIPS."
PHONE

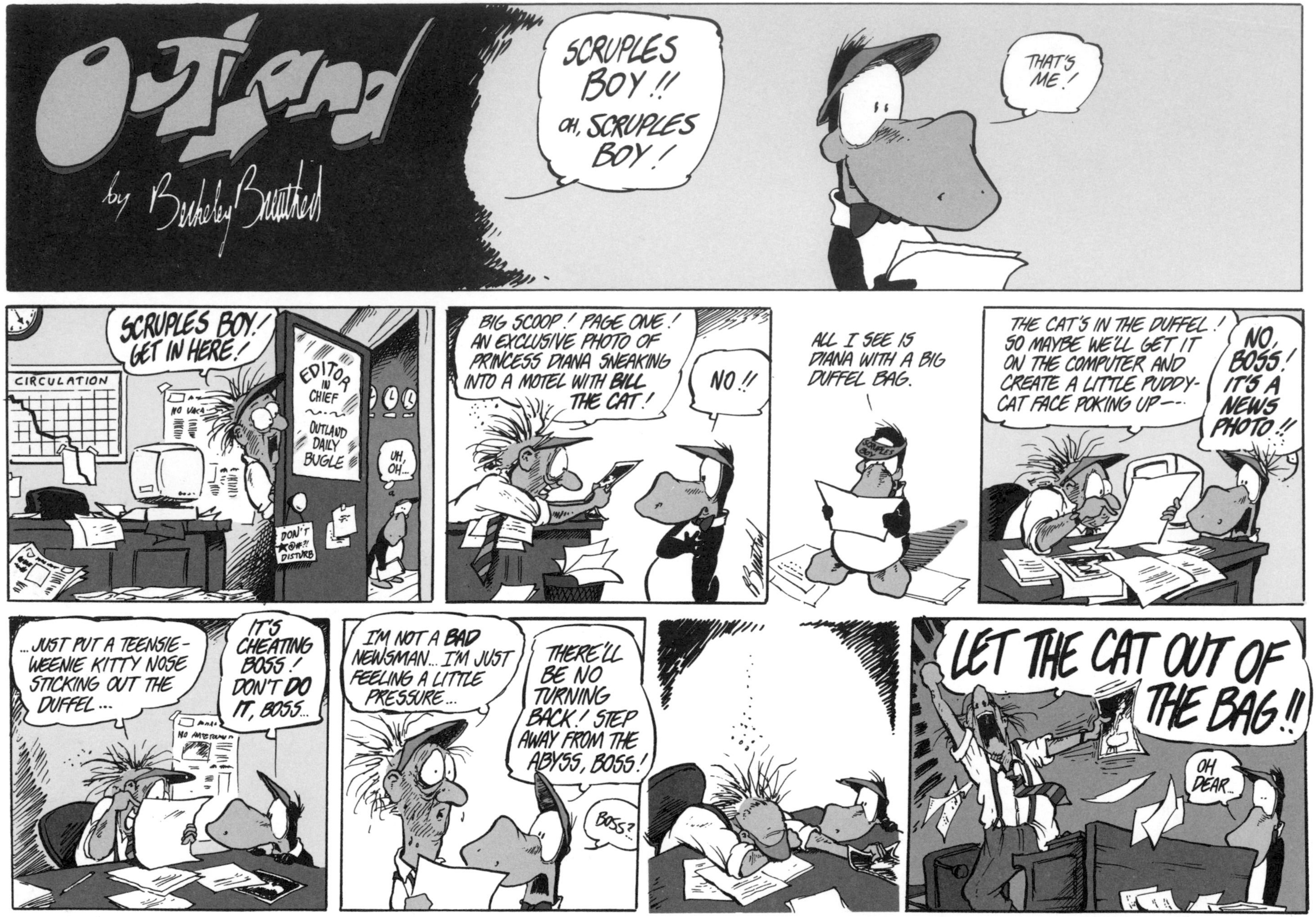

Outland
by Berkeley Breathed
SCRUPLES BOY!! OH, SCRUPLES BOY!
THAT'S ME!
SCRUPLES BOY! GET IN HERE!
CIRCULATION
NO VACA
EDITOR IN CHIEF
OUTLAND DAILY BUGLE
DON'T DISTURB
UH, OH...
BIG SCOOP! PAGE ONE! AN EXCLUSIVE PHOTO OF PRINCESS DIANA SNEAKING INTO A MOTEL WITH **BILL THE CAT**!
NO!!
ALL I SEE IS DIANA WITH A BIG DUFFEL BAG.
SCRUPLES BOY
THE CAT'S IN THE DUFFEL! SO MAYBE WE'LL GET IT ON THE COMPUTER AND CREATE A LITTLE PUDDY-CAT FACE POKING UP---
NO, BOSS! IT'S A NEWS PHOTO!!
...JUST PUT A TEENSIE-WEENIE KITTY NOSE STICKING OUT THE DUFFEL...
IT'S CHEATING BOSS! DON'T **DO** IT, BOSS...
I'M NOT A **BAD** NEWSMAN... I'M JUST FEELING A LITTLE PRESSURE...
THERE'LL BE NO TURNING BACK! STEP AWAY FROM THE ABYSS, BOSS!
BOSS?
LET THE CAT OUT OF THE BAG!!
OH DEAR...

Outland
by Berkeley Breathed
OH DRAT.
CREEEAK....
ANXIETY CLOSET
PSSST! LITTLE BOY! WANT SOME CANDY!?
ANXIETY CLOSET
HEE HEE!
...BRAIN CANDY! ...NUMBING, VIOLENT GAMES! CEASELESS ENTERTAINMENT! ...ENDLESS, MEANDERING CONVERSATIONS WITH STRANGERS!
COME, LITTLE BOY... STEP OUT ONTO THE HIGHWAY!...
...RIGHT INTO THE TRAFFIC!...
WHA—..? WHAT'S THAT?! PUT THAT AWAY!
BACK! GET BACK, YOU CEREBRUM-SUCKING DEMON FROM DIGITAL HELL!!
BINKLEY BEATS BACK THE FUTURE WITH "GREEN EGGS AND HAM"!
HA!
GREEN EGGS & HAM
YEP! WHAT ANXIETIES COULD THERE BE WITH A GOOD OL' LIBRARY BOOK?
1,733 WEEKS OVERDUE, DEAR.
BLOOM COUNTY 1982

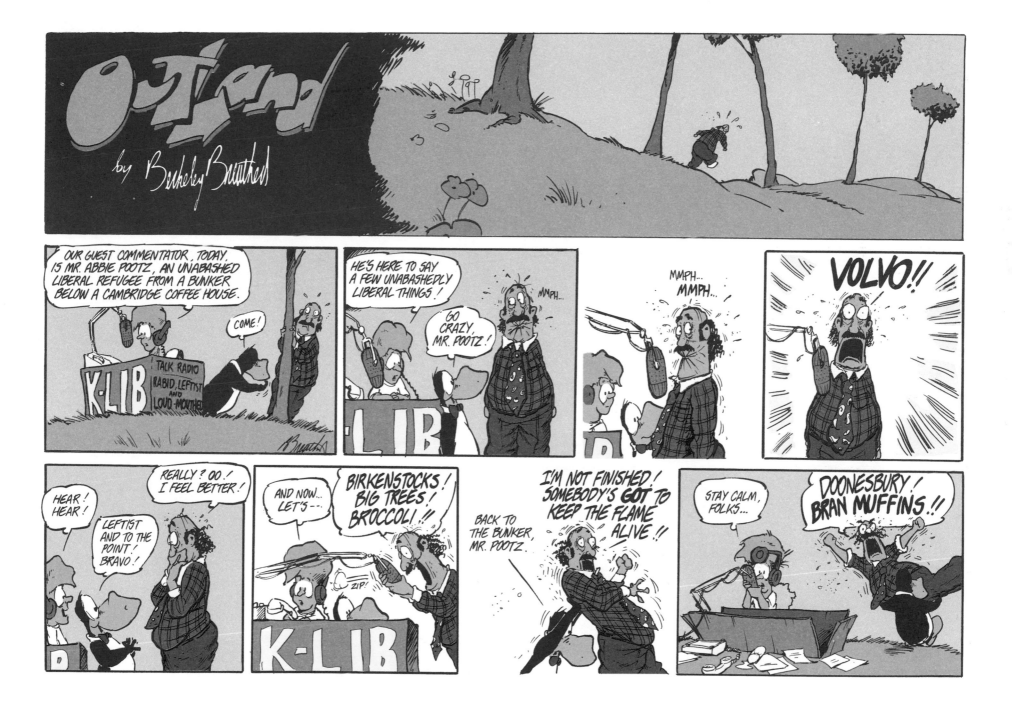

A few old favorites and a few old flops.
With a few words about them.

1.

$\mathcal{S}$hortly after my first effort at serious poetry hit the page in 1983, I received the following
note on the official stationery of the United States Secretary of Defense:

> *Dear Mr. Breathed,*
>
> *Many a morn I've longed to see*
> *A comic strip be kind to me.*
> *On 30 March, before my eyes*
> *A penguin watched a warm sunrise.*
> *In this land of so much bounty,*
> *Could I have that great Bloom County?*
>
> *Sincerely,*
> *Caspar Weinberger*

I sent it to him. Remember Caspar's letter when you are trying to get something from someone
who is not inclined to give it to you. All you need to know is here.

2.

eonard Nimoy sent the following after these strips appeared.

SIR:

LOGIC DICTATES THAT I COMMEND YOU ON YOUR CHARMING STRIP. THE
USE OF CHARACTERS FROM "STAR TREK" IS WELL DONE. WERE I HUMAN, I
WOULD BE FLATTERED.

LIVE LONG AND PROSPER,
SPOCK

What was interesting to me was the manner in which it was written. This was, after all, the man who wrote the defiant autobiography *I Am Not Spock*. Apparently he was mistaken.

But if he was a Vulcan, would he find anything "charming"? It's all confusing. I sent him the strip.

3.

To Kill a Mockingbird has had a relentless pull on me for twenty years. The story remains a fixture in my creative imagination, both the Pulitzer Prize–winning book by Harper Lee and the film. If there were a Mockingbird cult, I would be the little dweeb sending out the newsletter every month with illustrated instructions on how to make a Boo Radley costume.

I have often sprinkled references to the story throughout *Bloom County* and *Outland*, but it wasn't until I was actually going to mention Harper Lee's name that I thought I should try to contact the reclusive onetime author to ask permission. I figured if I didn't, she might see it and assume I was ridiculing her, as is my usual practice. *The horror.*

I wrote, not really knowing if she was still among the living. Months later arrived the most elegant letter I have ever received, postmarked from a distant backwater deep in the South. Ms. Lee confessed to what I had guessed: she prized privacy above all else. This precludes me from quoting her here, but she probably wouldn't mind my telling that the letter from the author of this century's most graceful novel was typed on an ancient Olivetti with a worn ribbon and a jumpy *r*. The smeared prose was embroidered with carefully erased typos and meticulously hand-crafted spelling corrections on Jurassic-era onion-skin typewriter paper. If it had been spat out spotless from an Apple computer, I would have thought the world slightly out of balance. I think she knew this.

The punchline is that she blessed my theft of her name. But the lasting detail remains the conclusion of her letter, signed simply and with casual Southern understatement, "Harper." Out of fondness, one hopes.

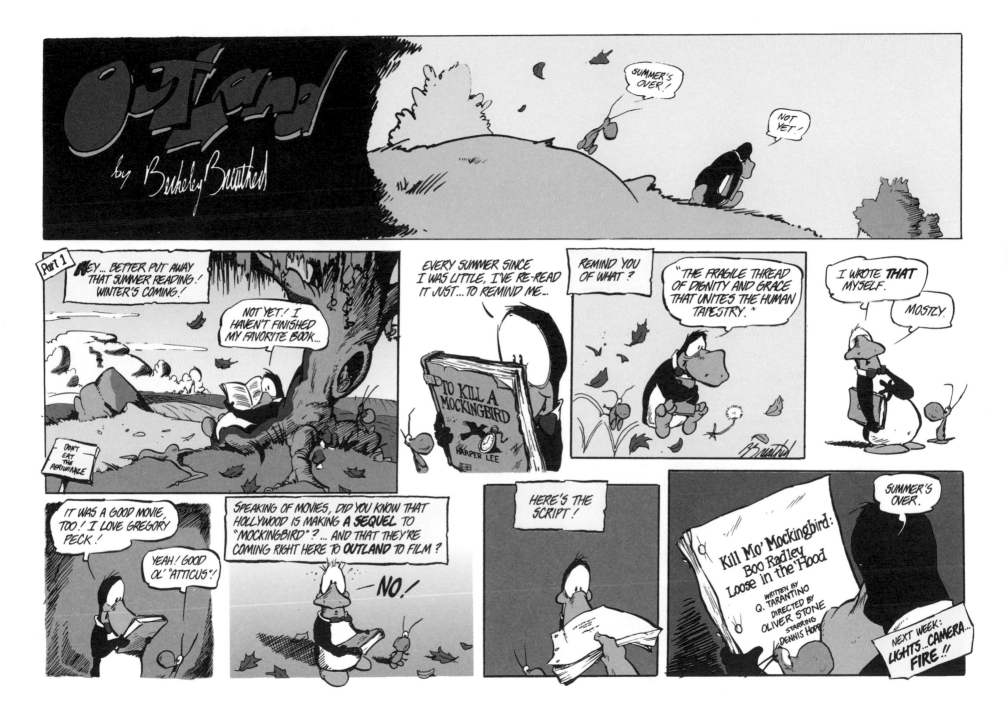

4.

Over the years I've traded communiqués with other cartoonists, with mixed results. *Doonesbury*'s Garry Trudeau never has forgiven me for building on his style during the early years and told me so in earnest, pointed notes. I'd feel more dismissive of them if I hadn't inadvertently lifted specific gags from his old strips that I'd absorbed as a kid, as his fans tirelessly point out to this day. I've included a particularly egregious sample from 1983, probably for the same therapeutic effect that inspires all those miserable wretches to cleanse their dirty laundry on the talk shows: redemption.

Now stop sending these to me.

DOONESBURY 1971

BLOOM COUNTY

5.

I have committed other thefts with a clean and unfettered conscience. *Garfield* was too calculated and too successful not to freely raid for illicit character cameos. *Calvin and Hobbes* was too *good* not to. *Calvin* creator Bill Watterson took these thefts in stride and retaliated in private with devastatingly effective illustrated salvos, hitting me in my most vulnerable places. Bill's sketch opposite is an editorial comment on my addiction to the expensive sport of powerboating and the moral compromises needed to fund it. That's me doing the kicking. The chap on the dock represents my cartoon syndicate boss, which says it all, methinks.

© Bill Watterson

6.

normally one steers clear of issues one has an emotional stake in. It usually makes for bad cartooning. I broke my own rule with testing on animals by Mary Kay Cosmetics. Only this once, I promised myself. Two weeks after the cartoons ran, I received a pink-paged autobiography and a letter (on pink, perfumed stationery) from the Grand Pink One herself, Mary Kay. She was nice, actually, in an understated, hint-of-legal-menace, pinkish sort of way. "I never dreamed," she wrote, "that one day we would be so well known that a cartoonist would devote cartoon after cartoon to us. YOU chose us — so we thank you!"

You're welcome!

Four weeks after that letter, the Mary Kay sales legions in the field were reporting grumbling from their clients, and Ms. Kay announced soon after that they would henceforth cease the needless testing of cosmetic acids on the eyes and skin of animals. But little time was spent gloating. Normally cartoonists have as little influence on matters of importance as Bill Clinton does. It's that bad.

7.

Gregory Peck was sent a copy of the strip opposite by his business-affairs person and replied to her the next day with the following, which she forwarded to me.

Dear Harriet,

Thank you for the warm note.
  What is Bloom County? What is the matter with me that I don't understand it?

> *Warmest regards,*
> *Gregory Peck*

Greg, my mother feels the same way.

8.

Opposite is one of the most heavily edited, lawyered, and cleansed strips I was ever to write. What was the problem, you ask? The lawyer-perceived suggestion that Jackson had minimal contact with women. The legal department of the *Washington Post* was catatonic over this. I found it all hugely fascinating. It was explained to me that we would be on the losing end of fortune-eating lawsuit if I were even to hint that a public figure was either of two things: a mobster or a homosexual(!).

Now, my meager intent with this particular strip was to suggest that Michael needed a date. This kept the lawyers working into the wee hours, stifling their panic and devising lawyerly doomsday scenarios for battling back a libel suit, despite the fact that at the time I needed a date *myself* and could hardly object if somebody else were to notice that fact. Fortunately somebody did, and she married me. Lisa Marie did the same to Michael. Everybody's obviously heterosexual. Lawyers . . . go figure.

9.

Opposite is the strip that prompted more mail and requests for reprints than any other in fifteen years. It also cost me a half dozen major newspapers. After three years, the loss of that syndication income is about $14,000. Cartoon martyrdom is an expensive but guilty pleasure.

10.

I'm always asked which strip of mine is my favorite. I've never known. Like I said, after I drew them, I rarely looked back. But this is the rare one that never fails to break me up when I come across it. Normally, one would never admit to laughing at one's own material. But then, if I don't laugh, even only occasionally, why bother?

Tuckus is my late father's term. He loved to appropriate multicultural vulgarities and found it immensely satisfying when they invariably showed up in *Bloom County*. He employed the verb *renoberate* frequently, which I also found to have a nicely resonant quality when coming from Opus's mouth. It means nothing, of course, which diminished its usefulness not a bit.

11.

Bill the Cat. This was his grand entrance. The gag, honestly, was to draw a cartoon character that had zero — or even minus — merchandising appeal . . . a character whose very saliva-dripping face would send hordes of consumers screaming from their mall gift stores. He didn't. I think there are lost Indian tribes in Venezuela that still wear penis sheaths made from some of the two million Bill the Cat T-shirts sold during the eighties.

This is probably why I didn't belong in cartooning.

12.

These are the particular strips that put Opus on the Funny Papers map. I had no intention of keeping the goofy little bird longer than the two weeks that he appeared. But after "Pear pimples for hairy fishnuts," the mail flowed in like warm penguin guano and I knew I had found the strip's center. A cartoonist is lucky if this happens even once in his or her career. The interesting thing is that you can't go looking for an Opus. You'll fail. Great characters aren't designed; they wander in from the street without knocking. Our job is to figure out which one should be cleaned up and given a hot bath. Then, of course, they never leave.

13.

On a sunny Iowa City Monday morning in 1983, I stepped out of the shower to answer the phone. A voice said, "Please hold for the President." I held, waiting, and then not really knowing the social protocol for such things, I stood at attention, naked. Ronald Reagan picked up the phone and told me in his charmingly deferential manner how pleased he was with that Sunday's *Bloom County*. This threw me briefly, because it hadn't been about anything he should be particularly interested in, except that I had included a small portrait of Nancy Reagan hanging in the background of one of the panels. It was a photocopy of a young Nancy, but he apparently assumed it was the world's first flattering caricature of the woman he worshipped. Would you like the original strip, I asked the planet's most powerful man. Oh, he said, "I didn't think you fellas gave those things away."

There is, I said, a short list of people to whom we give them away, and you are somewhere on it.

Some months later, this gesture earned me a trip to Washington for a White House dinner for the president of Afghanistan. Or was it Algeria. I know it was an "A" country where women wear flamingo-pink see-through harem pants, because the president's wife was wearing such a pair. Not Nancy, the other one. Someday I'll tell that whole Reagan dinner story, but all I can tell you now is that it included lots of 3-x-5 cards, an argument with Mrs. Reagan about the general use-fulness of comic strips, a pickled Joe Namath, and Secretary of State George Schultz nuzzling the earlobe of a former Charlie's Angel on the dance floor.

To this day, when I think back on that conversation with the Commander in Chief during a sunny Iowa Monday morning, I regret not saying, "Sir, I should tell you that I am not wearing any pants."

14.

*I*n 1986 I had a nasty landing in an ultralight aircraft and managed to crumple my spinal column. This was a bad week for aviation, as the *Challenger* blew up a few days later. I recall little about that time except the disappearance of my usual self-pity as I watched the video of the shuttle fireball play repeatedly on the intensive care unit television above my head.

I took a couple of months off from stripping and then came back to the page with my recent adventures retold through my alter ego, Steve Dallas. Fortunately, my fiancée, Jody, was far more forgiving than Steve's — forgiving enough to marry me some months later while I was in exactly the same body brace as the one I drew on Mr. Dallas. Our hero's surgeon, Dr. LeGrunt, is a barely disguised caricature of the extremely shy and extremely skilled Dr. LeGant, the man who wired my back together. I don't think he was much amused by all the public attention and probably regretted not wiring my drawing hand to my vertebrae when he had the chance.

15.

Dogs. At the Breathed house there be more than a few. But no children, which causes the in-laws consternation, for they see little logic in an author of four children's picture books having no test audience at hand. The reason is self-evident: dogs will never wear their trousers pulled down around their knees in public. Or at least if they do, we can discipline them without getting sued. Seems a valuable distinction at this point. I urge anybody to trade in their teenager toward a schnauzer mix.

So dog/person relationships sneak into my cartoons where kid/parent relationships normally go. Not surprisingly, I am particularly fond of these.

16.

I admire dogs for reasons that I have consistently explored in my cartoons: they know how to kick back and contemplate things. This time-out for simple reflection is an essential activity that is — like bowling and casual sex — slowly disappearing from modern life. This has always been of some concern to me, and you see it in the frequent return of my characters to places like Milo's Meadow and the Dandelion Patch. It is a notion that seemed to strike a resonant chord with many of you out there. And while I myself may not be found actually Lying Naked in the Periwinkle, I may be found fully clothed on a motorcycle in the desert or on a boat in Alaska . . . my private, mobile Dandelion Patches. You'll agree that Opus seems to fit better atop fresh flowers than on a Harley-Davidson.

17.

*C*utter John: my Vietnam vet characters before Vietnam vet characters became tricky clichés. Cutter was tricky in a way illustrated by an exchange I had with a disabled woman after a campus speech some years ago. She wanted to know why she hadn't seen Cutter John in the strip recently. I answered her too honestly, probably: I said that fitting a character who is always sitting down into the same frame with other standing characters proved frustrating enough to possibly steer my imagination to ideas easier drawn. She responded, of course, by suggesting that I ought to try sitting in a wheelchair myself for real frustration.

Her response was proper and my chagrin deserved. Still, it highlights the problem of such characters: they cannot be released from their victim status to work smoothly and unself-consciously in a comic ensemble. So Cutter John eventually lost my interest. Still, the strips opposite proved great fun to draw, and I hold fond thoughts for Cutter and the Critters.

The Sunday panel opposite, by the way, was written during one of the formerly discussed 4:00 A.M. semicomatose, hallucinogenic 'tooning sessions. It shocks me that thirteen years later, I — well rested, mentally alert, and finally nearing adulthood — still find the line "space walrus with photon flippers or something" serviceably funny. If you do too, then this book has found a friend and I haven't wasted nearly two decades.